THE FUNDAMENTALS OF
OIL PAINTING

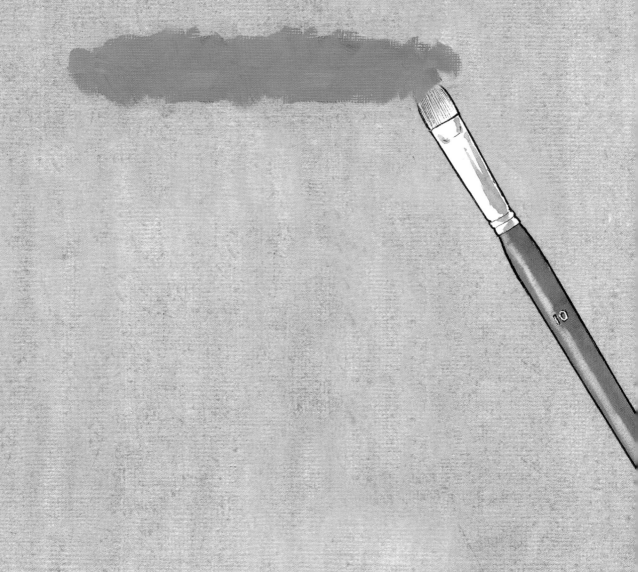

THE FUNDAMENTALS OF
OIL PAINTING

A COMPLETE COURSE IN TECHNIQUES, SUBJECTS, AND STYLES

Barrington Barber

ARCTURUS

ARCTURUS

This edition first published in 2014 by Arcturus Publishing

Distributed by Black Rabbit Books
P.O. Box 3263
Mankato
Minnesota MN 56002

Library of Congress Cataloging-in-Publication Data

Barber, Barrington.
 The fundamentals of oil painting : a complete course in techniques, subjects, and styles / Barrington Barber.
     pages cm. -- (Creative workshop)
 Includes index.
 Summary: "Instructs readers about techniques, materials and projects for oil painting"--Provided by publisher.
 ISBN 978-1-78212-411-5 (library binding)
 1. Painting--Technique--Juvenile literature. I. Title.
 ND1146.B36 2014
 751.45--dc23
                              2013004696

Printed in China

SL003589US
Supplier 02, Date 0613, Print Run 2390

CONTENTS

CHAPTER 1

MATERIALS AND COLORS

In this section we look at everything you will require to begin painting in oils, including brushes, supports, easels, and of course colors, along with an understanding of their relationships with each other.

The multifarious things that may be found in an artist's studio are so extensive in range that you could spend enormous amounts of money acquiring them all, only to discover that you use just a few of them. In this chapter I describe the items that you will need to make a start, and only when you know a little more about what you are doing should you think about extending your range of materials.

You can paint with very little, so long as you have pigments, brushes, and a surface on which to paint. Even an easel is not entirely necessary, although if you take up oil painting seriously you will probably want one. It is worth spending a reasonable amount of money on the most important pieces of equipment, because the better materials last longer and feel better to use than the very cheapest. However, if you do buy the cheapest you will find you can still paint quite well—although you may have to replace them more often, making them quite not as economical as they seem at first.

A little knowledge of color values and how they work in painting is not difficult to master, and your handling of color will become more subtle as you progress. Eventually, mixing colors becomes almost automatic and you will be surprised by just how effective your use of them becomes.

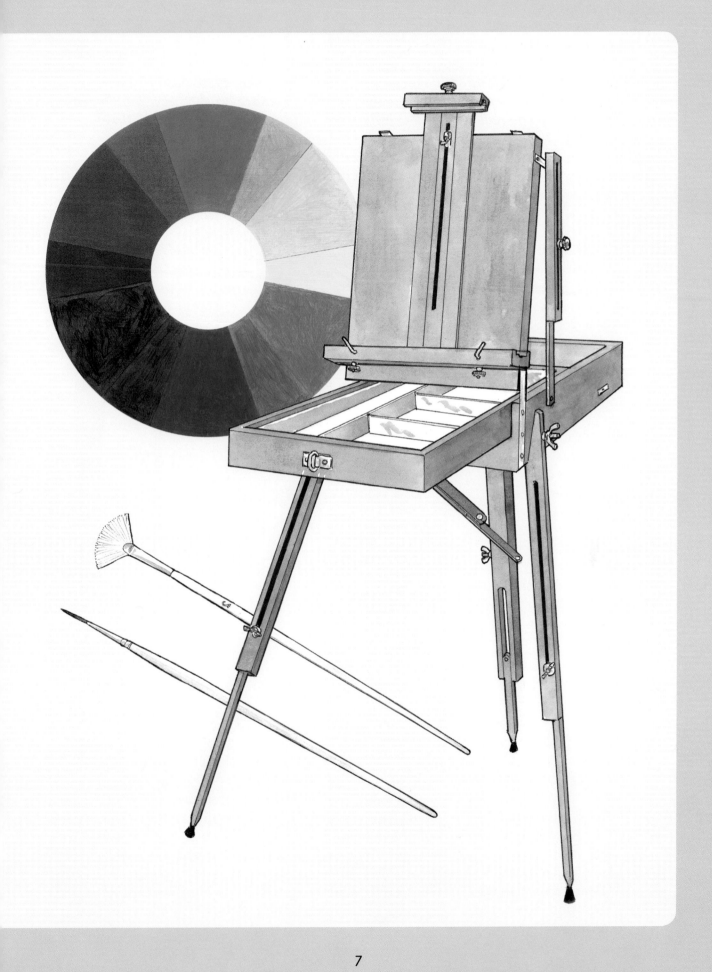

BRUSHES

While oil paintings can be done entirely with bristle brushes, it's useful to have softer brushes too for detail or for subtle areas where you want to reduce brushmarks. You'll need quite a few brushes if you really get into painting, but you can build them up over time.

Buying cheaper brushes can be a false economy as the better types tend to last much longer, so it's best to buy good-quality brushes from the outset if possible and look after them carefully (see box). Here is my basic list of brushes, which will be more than enough to get you started.

Bristle Brushes

These are usually made from hog's hair, though synthetic ones, which are normally softer, are also available. They come in a range of styles, each with its own use.

Flats

Flat brushes have a flattened set of bristles, rather like a refined version of a decorator's brush. They are the brushes you'll use most of the time, as they hold the paint well and you can apply it to your canvas using both the wide surface and the edge to get varying brush marks. The following sizes are a useful range: 20 (probably the largest you will need unless you wish to paint murals), 12, 10, 8, 4, 2, and 1.

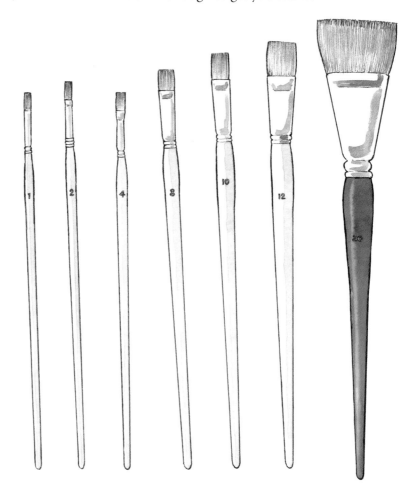

Cleaning Brushes

To clean brushes, first wipe off any excess paint with a sheet of paper towel or rag, squeezing from the ferrule downward but taking care not to pull on the bristles. Rinse them in solvent first to get the paint out of the hairs—you can push hog's hair brushes about in the solvent, but you must be much gentler with sables or they will lose their point. Wash them in liquid soap and cold water to clean out the solvent and any remaining paint. Once you're sure they are clean, give them a final rinse in water. Reshape the brushes gently with your fingers and leave to dry. Never stand them upright resting on their bristles as this will destroy the shape.

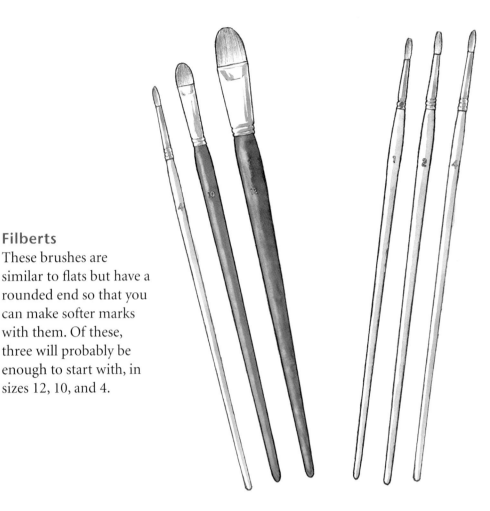

Filberts

These brushes are similar to flats but have a rounded end so that you can make softer marks with them. Of these, three will probably be enough to start with, in sizes 12, 10, and 4.

Rounds

As you might expect from the name, these brushes are rounded down the whole length of the bristles. They can be very useful because they are capable of holding more paint, allowing you to pile it on more easily. They are also good for scumbling, as the bristles spread out in all directions. You will need sizes 4, 2, and 1.

Soft Brushes

The best soft brushes are made from sable hair, but if your budget is tight the cheaper brushes made from squirrel, ox, or synthetic hair are very acceptable. I recommend you have one large brush, size 12, and three in sizes 4, 1, and 0; these smaller brushes are ideal for the very fine marks that you might wish to make in the final stages of your painting.

Soft brushes for oil painting have longer handles than those for watercolor, partly so that you can keep your hands away from the wet paint, but also to enable you to stand back from your painting.

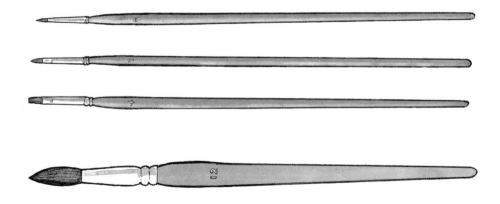

Other Brushes

Once you begin painting you may find that some brushmarks are too difficult to make without more specialized brushes, so the following three types of brush are worth considering.

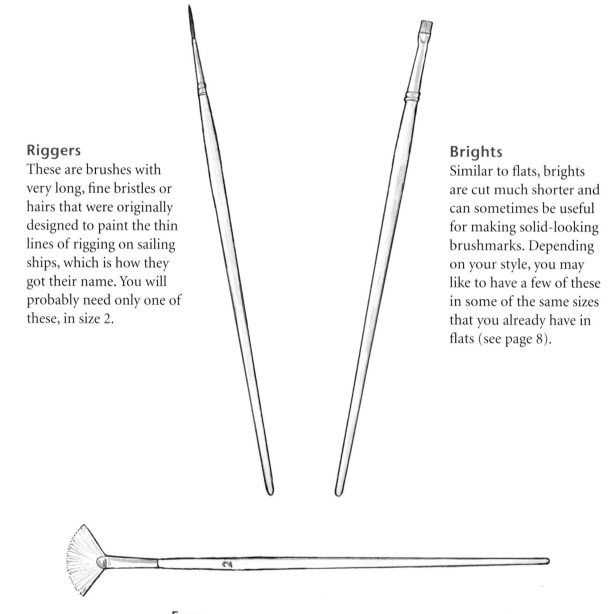

Riggers

These are brushes with very long, fine bristles or hairs that were originally designed to paint the thin lines of rigging on sailing ships, which is how they got their name. You will probably need only one of these, in size 2.

Brights

Similar to flats, brights are cut much shorter and can sometimes be useful for making solid-looking brushmarks. Depending on your style, you may like to have a few of these in some of the same sizes that you already have in flats (see page 8).

Fans

Fan-shaped brushes are ideal for softening the edges of your painted marks. Just one, in size 2, should suffice.

PALETTE KNIVES

There are quite a few variations of size and shape in the range of palette knives available, but unless you're going to do a lot of knife painting, two will be enough. Of those shown here, the one with the larger blade (right) is very useful for cleaning palettes and mixing large amounts of paint. The smaller blade (below) is good for mixing paint (rather than using your brush) and is also the best type for applying paint to the canvas if you need thicker marks. With just these two you can do most of the techniques shown in this book.

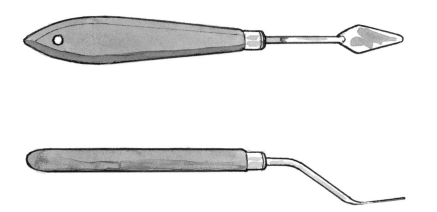
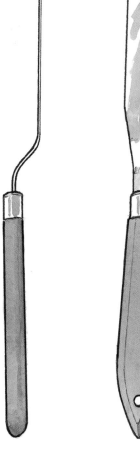

MAHL STICK

A mahl stick is a device that painters have used for many centuries to steady the hand when painting details in a picture. Some art stores sell them, but it is easy enough to make your own: just pad out a piece of cloth or soft leather into a ball as shown and tie it tightly to the end of a straight stick. This gives you a support on which to rest your painting wrist (see page 28).

PALETTES

You can buy many kinds of palette, but essentially they are all just a flat surface on which you can keep all your colors. The traditional palette is shaped in an ellipse with a hole for the thumb and a deep curve cut into the side, which enables the painter to hold the palette with one hand and the brush or palette knife with the other. Nowadays palettes come in many shapes, often rectangular or round, and usually with a thumbhole.

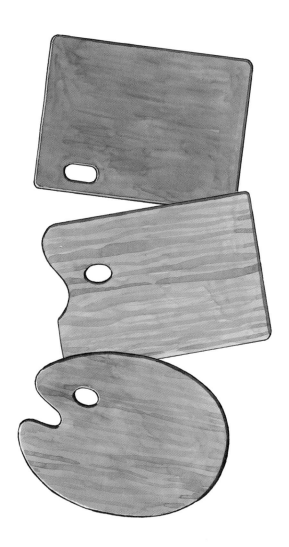

I often have my palette lying flat on a surface next to me, so the shape doesn't matter—all that's needed is a surface that will not soak up the paint, and most heavily varnished boards can be used in this way. Some artists use glass or plastic surfaces to mix paint on, so you can experiment and see which you prefer.

Disposable palettes come in pads of several sizes and can be useful, if eventually rather expensive; you simply tear off a palette sheet and tape it to your work surface. Tracing paper or waterproof paper will work equally well. In my view, a hard palette feels nicer and lasts for a long time, but if you have limited time in which to clear up, or if you are trying to cut down on weight when working on location, you may find a disposable palette practical to use.

PAINTS

Some artists mix their own paints from raw pigment, but the quality of the paint sold in tubes, ready to use, is good enough for most people. The most common sizes are 1.25 fl oz (37ml), 5 fl oz (150ml) or 6.75 fl oz (200ml) . The former should be adequate for most colors, though it's worth buying white in a larger size. The larger sizes are much more economical.

I always use oil paints ready-mixed with alkyd medium, which speeds up the rate of drying. I often want to paint over dried paint, and as alkyd oil paint dries in about 6–12 hours, I can paint again after leaving it overnight. If this is not something you want to do then traditional oil paint will be fine, but it does take a good while longer to dry; exactly how long will depend on the color, how thickly you have applied it, as well as which medium you have used.

The names of the colors given in this book are for the pigments I use, but you should be able to find near equivalents in all manufacturers' ranges. Conveniently, color charts can be found on the manufacturers' websites on the Internet.

THINNERS

The most commonly used thinner for oil paint is turpentine. This is not the ordinary household turps, which will affect the colors of the paint, but refined distilled turpentine, which is usually sold only in art stores. It does have a strong smell, and if you don't like it you can get low-odor substitutes such as Sansodor. Some people are allergic to turpentine, so if you are painting in a group or using a model it is always best to use a substitute.

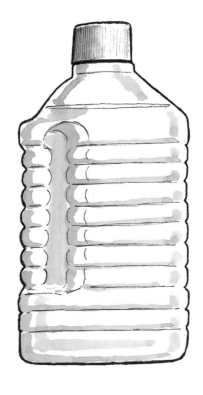

MEDIUMS

The most popular medium is linseed oil; for the best effects use the refined, cold-pressed version. It will add considerable oiliness to your paint, and I don't use it myself because the paint in the tube has enough oil in it already as far as I'm concerned. All mediums are a matter of personal choice and you will find a range offering different qualities in most art supplies stores, such as Liquin, which gives a very smooth layer of paint and is good for glazes (see page 39). It also contains dryers that help the paint to dry quickly.

VARNISH

The main purpose of a varnish is to protect the painting, but it also harmonizes the surface quality of the paint so that you don't see matt and shiny surfaces next to each other. Varnishes are sold in both gloss and matt finish, depending on the effect you wish to achieve. You can also buy retouching varnish, which is particularly good if you wish to work on a painting again at a later stage. It allows the new paint to bind with the dried paint more effectively and helps to prevent cracking (see page 28).

CANVAS AND BOARD

The most traditional surfaces to paint on in oil are canvas and boards of different kinds. The great advantage of canvas is that it is very light to handle and can be easily transported and stored. It is stretched tightly across a wooden frame and then pinned to it with either staples or small nails. In the inside corners at the back of the canvas are slots that wooden wedges can be tapped into with a small hammer to stretch the canvas even tighter (see below). The surface of the canvas must be as taut as possible in order to paint on it easily.

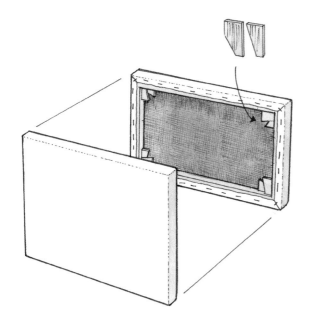

When you buy ready-stretched canvases in art stores, they are already sized and coated with a white primer that provides a good surface for painting. Many painters like to stretch and prepare their own canvases, but I suggest that until you have some experience, buying stretched canvases is a sensible practice as you can begin to paint right away. You can buy many cheap and well-made canvases in a variety of sizes. When you feel ready to do so, you can then progress to stretching more expensive fabrics.

Canvas boards, which are simply canvas glued to a stiff board, are also a very useful surface for painting, and they don't take up quite so much room as canvases on wooden stretchers.

It's also possible to paint on a type of canvas paper available from art stores. You may find this a good way to start oil painting because it is easy to put away at the end of a session, having no more bulk than a thick sheet of paper. It is also much easier to dispose of if you don't like your first attempts! The paper is textured to simulate primed canvas and is usually sold in large and small pads, like a sketchbook, but can also be bought in single sheets.

A very economical way to make your own painting surface is to buy pieces of medium density fiberboard (MDF) or good plywood board from a timber yard or DIY store. They come in a variety of thicknesses, any of which are suitable for your purposes, though of course the added weight of the thicker board makes it less practical.

You will need to prepare the surface—back, front, and edges—with acrylic gesso, which is a thick, white painting medium that coats board very well; several coats may be required to achieve a surface that is good to paint on and to protect the board from damp, which causes warping. Sanding with fine sandpaper helps to smooth the surface.

The only drawback to these painting surfaces is that they are much heavier than canvas and are therefore not so easy to transport. Wooden boards were the traditional way of painting until the Renaissance period, when canvas became more popular—as you can imagine, a large painting on solid wood would have been very heavy and difficult to move around.

EASELS

You don't need an easel in order to start painting, but it does make life easier; it enables you to keep your studio space much cleaner, and your painting can be left on the easel to dry in safety. I like radial easels (see right), which are sturdy enough to support most canvases and give a very firm base to work on, with the advantage that they are easily folded up to put away or carry to a new venue.

Another easel that you might like to invest in is a box easel, which is the best kind of truly portable easel—most other types are very fiddly to put up and are so flimsy that they fall over at the least pressure. The box easel has an area in which to put paints and, beneath that, compartments for brushes. It also has space in which to secure small canvases or canvas boards. The only piece of equipment that it doesn't accommodate easily is thinner or medium, but this can be carried in a small bag hung from the shoulder. The box easel folds up quite neatly to about the size of a small suitcase. I use one of these whenever I am painting outdoors as it is so easy to transport.

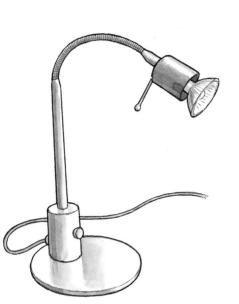

LIGHTING

Good lighting is essential for an artist, and the ideal is a studio with a window in the ceiling or a north-facing window high in a wall, to give an even light, with plenty of directional artificial lighting available as well. You may not be lucky enough to have the ideal situation, but that needn't stop you painting.

In my studio I have good artificial lighting so that I can work late at night if necessary. Apart from overhead lights, I have a couple of small spotlights so that I can adjust the angle of light to my needs, but a small directional lamp would do just as well.

COLOR THEORY

In order to use colors effectively in your paintings you need to understand at least the basics of color theory. Color is never seen in isolation—we always perceive it in relation to another color, or in relation to white or black. For the purposes of artists, colors are generally shown arranged in the form of a wheel to make it easier to see their relationships.

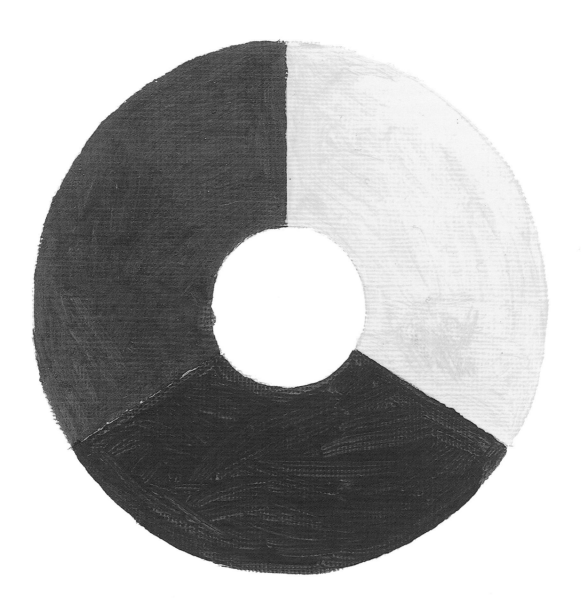

Primary Colors

This wheel shows the three primary colors: red, blue, and yellow. All other colors are made by mixing together the primary colors, but the primary colors themselves cannot be achieved by mixing.

Secondary Colors

The colors made by mixing two primary colors together are called the secondary colors. In this color wheel (right), they are shown between the primaries from which they are derived. Blue mixed with red makes purple; red mixed with yellow makes orange; and yellow mixed with blue makes green.

The colors immediately opposite each other across the wheel are called complementary colors—red and green are complementary, blue and orange are complementary, and yellow and purple are complementary.

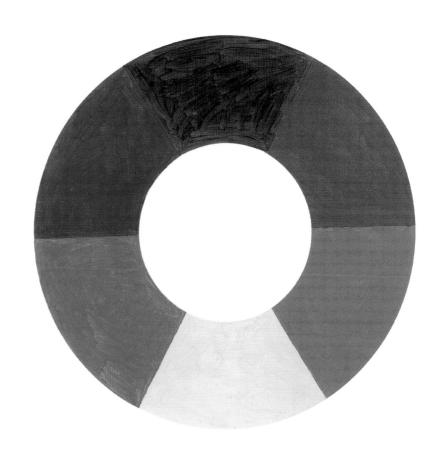

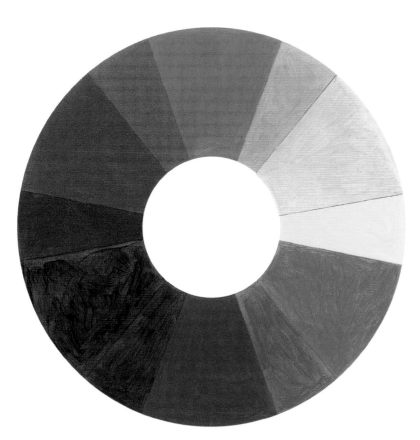

Tertiary Colors

The tertiary colors are mixtures of the primary colors with the secondary colors. This extended color wheel (left) shows the secondary colors between the primaries, and the tertiary colors either side of the secondaries.

By mixing primary and secondary colors, you can make all the variations in colors that you need, sometimes with the addition of white to reduce their darkness. This is how you will make all your neutral colors—grays and browns (see page 24).

BASIC COLOR RANGES

The first colors that you will need are of course the three primary colors. For the yellow, I suggest Cadmium Yellow Light (or Pale); for the red, Cadmium Red Light; and for the blue, French Ultramarine. As you can see, these are very clear colors and are a good base from which to start.

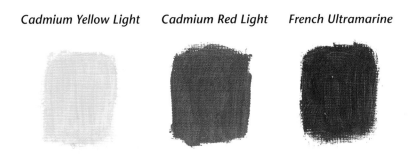

Cadmium Yellow Light   *Cadmium Red Light*   *French Ultramarine*

However, to mix all the subtle variations that are possible you will also need to buy variations on these primaries. I recommend Cadmium Lemon and Naples Yellow to open out the yellow range, Alizarin Crimson and Vermilion to open out the red range, and Cerulean Blue and Dioxazine Purple (which is really a violet) to open out the blue range.

Cadmium Lemon   *Alizarin Crimson*   *Cerulean Blue*

Naples Yellow   *Vermilion*   *Dioxazine Purple*

18

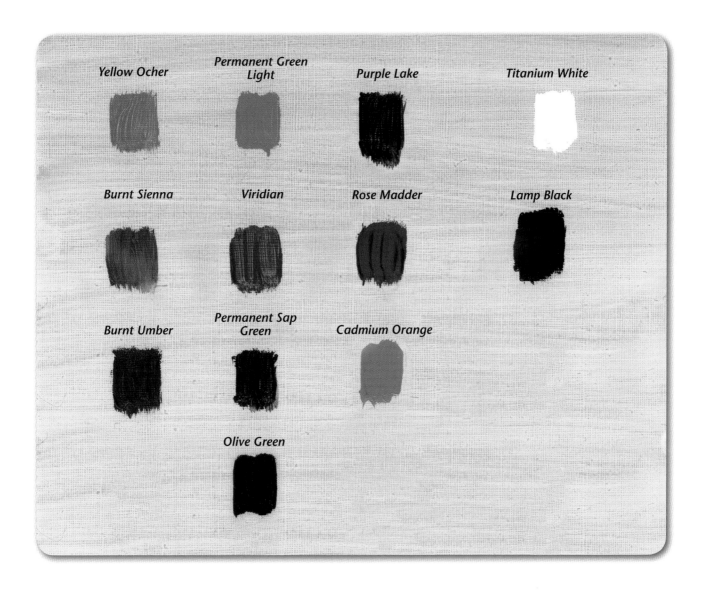

Even with this range of ready-made colors you will still need to mix most of the colors that you wish to paint with, so a few more will be helpful: for browns, Yellow Ocher, Burnt Sienna, and Burnt Umber; for greens, Permanent Green Light, Viridian, Permanent Sap Green, and Olive Green; Purple Lake, mainly for mixing with other colors to get interesting tones; Rose Madder as a softer version of Alizarin Crimson; and Cadmium Orange to strengthen warm colors. Of course, no range of colors would be complete without white and black, so I suggest Titanium White and Lamp Black as two good versions of these. There is a huge range of other tempting colors available, but I find these are all I need.

COLOR TEMPERATURE

When we look at colors, the brain interprets what we see as being either warm or cool. Traditionally, the warm colors are reds, oranges, and yellows (the color of fire and the sun), plus the warmer browns; the cold colors are blues and blue-grays and some blueish-greens. However, to make things a bit more complicated, some cool colors tend toward warm and some warm ones tend toward cold. Yellow is generally seen as warm, for example, but with the addition of some green to create a more acidic lemony color it can be seen as cooler; if, however, you make it a little more orange it becomes warmer since it is closer to red.

Below are colors with examples of warm, intermediate, and cold values.

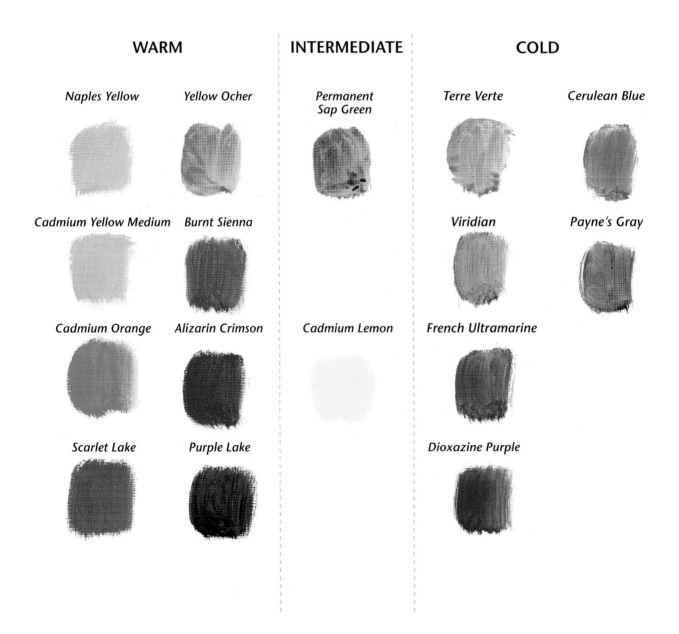

WARM		INTERMEDIATE	COLD	
Naples Yellow	Yellow Ocher	Permanent Sap Green	Terre Verte	Cerulean Blue
Cadmium Yellow Medium	Burnt Sienna		Viridian	Payne's Gray
Cadmium Orange	Alizarin Crimson	Cadmium Lemon	French Ultramarine	
Scarlet Lake	Purple Lake		Dioxazine Purple	

Shadow and Light

When you're painting scenes with strong light cast over them, you'll find that where the light is warm the shadows will appear cooler and, conversely, with a cool light the shadows will be warmer. Conveying this will help enormously to give greater depth and vibrancy to the picture.

Warm Light, Cool Shadows

In this painting of the entrance to Menelaus's tomb at Therapne, the landscape seen through the opening is bathed in sunlight. The outside is painted in hot yellow tones, to give the effect of Mediterranean sunlight. Inside the dark tomb the shadows are strong blues, with a touch of violet and green. These colder colors contrast with the colors of the outside, emphasizing their warmth.

Cold Light, Warm Shadows

Here a runner is just finishing a race, and the predominant light colors are cool, pale blues, and white with a hint of green. The shadows on the runner's neck and tunic are in warm brownish-yellows and purple. Again the effect is a strong feeling of the open air, with cool light in contrast to the warm, dark tones on the figure.

Other Color Terminology

You may also come across other terms used in relation to colors (see below). If you find them rather confusing, don't be concerned—you will gradually get to know them in conversation with other artists, and your skill doesn't depend on knowing all the right terminology.

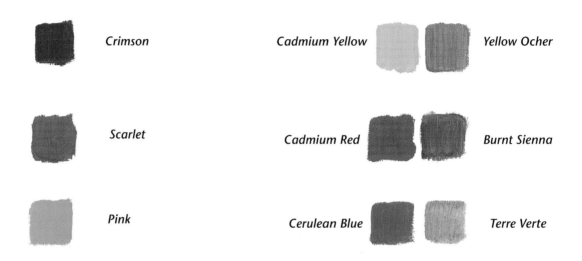

Crimson

Cadmium Yellow   Yellow Ocher

Scarlet

Cadmium Red   Burnt Sienna

Pink

Cerulean Blue   Terre Verte

Hue

This simply describes colors by name, such as red, yellow, or blue. Crimson, scarlet, and pink all have a red hue, for example.

Intensity

Some colors have greater intensity than others, and really leap out of a painting. For example, Cadmium Yellow has a strong intensity, whereas Yellow Ocher is more subdued; Cadmium Red and Cerulean Blue both have strong intensity, whereas Burnt Sienna and Terre Verte both have less.

Vermilion

Titanium White and Alizarin Crimson

French Ultramarine

Lamp Black and Burnt Sienna

Tone

When you paint unmixed colors onto a surface, some look lighter or darker than others. For example, French Ultramarine is quite dark in tone, whereas Vermilion is much lighter.

Tints and Shades

Tints are made mostly by mixing white with a color to produce a lighter color. Shades are the opposite, where black mixed with a color produces a darker version of that color.

SETTING OUT YOUR PALETTE

When you lay out your palette at the start of a painting session, always begin with the colors that you know you will need—others can be added as work progresses. It's a good idea to put the same colors in the same place on the palette for each session, as this makes it easier to find them without thinking about it too much.

Let's take the example of painting a figure from life. Before starting a life painting I prepare a canvas with a thin layer of Burnt Sienna, because I don't like to paint on a white canvas (see page 30). When this is dry I can begin to lay out my palette to start painting. The palette below is specifically focused on painting figures from life, but it could also be used for portraiture.

On the left-hand side, I place a range of colors that I find useful for basic color and tone. Starting at the bottom left and working upward and around the outer edge of the palette, I place Naples Yellow, then Yellow Ocher, Burnt Sienna, and Burnt Umber. This gives me most of the basic warm colors I need.

Then, leaving a small gap, I put a little Flesh Tint, which is a warm light pink, and then some Permanent Alizarin Crimson. These give me all the really warm colors I require, but I don't need much of them.

Now, over on the right-hand side of the palette, nearest to the Alizarin Crimson, I put some Purple Lake or Dioxazine Purple. Next to that I put some French Ultramarine, which is a marvellous blue that gives all the colder tints that I might want. It's very strong and I don't use much of it on the figure itself, but it can be useful to build up a tonal background.

At the bottom right-hand edge, I put a little Viridian—a very cool green that can be useful for cool tones on flesh.

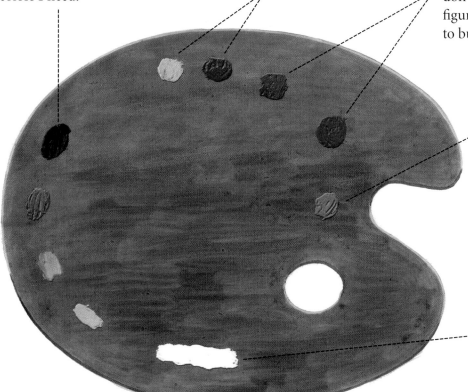

Along the bottom edge of the palette, I usually place a large sweep of Titanium White for mixing and lightening all the other colors.

MIXING COMPLEMENTARY COLORS

In order to make some subtle grays and browns to balance out your color range, while retaining a harmonious quality to the mixtures, it is best to use complementary mixes of colors rather than buying ready-mixed tubes. To do this, mix the colors that appear on opposite sides of the color wheel (see page 17). Here you can see what happens when you mix these complementary colors together.

Begin by mixing French Ultramarine and Cadmium Orange to produce the type of dark gray shown. However, this will probably be too dark in tone for most uses, so mix in some white to make the next gray tone. Add even more white to make the gray softer and lighter still, and you can see this last color has quite a nice feel to it.

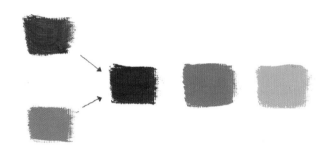

Now try Permanent Green Light and Cadmium Red Light mixed together. The result is a warm dark brown. Add some white and the tone gets lighter; add even more white for a lovely yellowish color.

Next try mixing Dioxazine Purple and Cadmium Yellow Light. Again you get a strong, brownish color. Add some white for a more grayish tone; add yet more white and the tone becomes even more subtle.

Mix of Cadmium Orange, French Ultramarine, and Titanium White

More Orange   More Blue

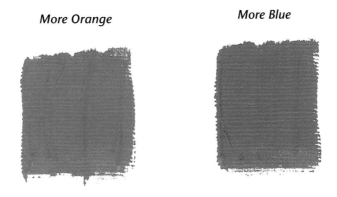

Mix of Permanent Green Light, Cadmium Red Light, and Titanium

More Green   More Red

Mix of Dioxazine Purple, Cadmium Yellow Light, and Titanium White

More Purple   More Yellow

These colors can, of course, be changed slightly by adding more of each of the colors used in the mixes, as shown here. It is worth trying out all these mixes on a large piece of canvas board or canvas paper so that you can see all the variations together. This is how you begin to understand just how many subtle color variations can be made, even with a very restricted palette.

CHAPTER 2

METHODS OF WORK

Once you have your equipment, you can explore how to apply the paint to your work surface and manipulate it successfully. There are many ways to do this, but we will stick to the most commonly used methods, which are the simplest and most effective.

Before you start painting, it's wise to lay what is known as a "ground"—an overall color, usually in a midtone, so that you are not trying to work out the balance of tones against the white of the canvas. We shall look at the thinking behind the colors that you might want to choose for you picture, before going on to consider whether to draw your subject in charcoal or with a brush, and then to look at the choice of painting techniques that lend themselves to oils. You will discover how to mix, darken, and lighten colors, how to lay thin glazes and heavy impasto, and how to work with palette knives, among other time-honored methods.

We shall also discuss how to use the technique of "squaring up" to transfer a small work made on location to a much larger scale, such as might be used for a studio painting.

USING YOUR EQUIPMENT

Once you have assembled the equipment discussed in the previous chapter you will be keen to begin painting. However, before you do so, it's worth taking a little time to make sure you are going about things the right way in order to avoid wasting both time and money.

Painting in oils can be quite messy, and it's a good idea to have some protection for your clothes before you even start opening tubes of paint and bottles of medium. Most painters wear coveralls, an apron, or just their oldest, most battered clothes, which they reserve for painting.

To clean brushes as you are painting, you need a plentiful supply of clean rags or paper towels, so save old sheets or shirts to tear up and use for paint rags.

The Mahl Stick

This is an aid for painting careful detail, when it's particularly important that your hand doesn't slip or wobble. Place the mahl stick across the painting, held in your left hand if you are right-handed or vice versa, with the ball end resting on the side of the canvas or on the easel itself. Then, with your hand resting on the stick part, you can paint very small details with a steady hand.

Retouching Varnish

This varnish allows you to return to a painting that is dry and add further paint without the likelihood of it flaking off in a few years' time. Prop up the canvas at an angle of about 45 degrees and spread the varnish across the painting with a soft, wide brush, starting at the top and working horizontally across the canvas until you reach the bottom. Leave for about an hour to allow the varnish to dry and you can then apply the fresh paint, which will bind with the paint already present. The varnish is very liquid, so be careful of using too much.

It's best to have a separate brush for varnishing, though it's not essential. Clean the brush in the same way as paintbrushes (see page 8). Since varnish is clear it is harder to see if the brush is clean, so you need to be especially thorough.

Masking Tape

When you want to paint a hard straight edge, such as in an abstract painting, you can use masking tape to obtain it more easily.

Begin by laying down the tape to isolate the area of new color that you want to paint (see below). Press down firmly on the edge of the tape closest to the color, because it's possible for the paint to creep under the masking tape, especially if it's very liquid.

Then, with a broad brush, apply the paint until the whole area is covered.

When the paint is dry enough (touch dry is sufficient), carefully peel off the masking tape to reveal an area of color with a clean, straight edge. If any tiny flecks of paint have crept under the tape, just touch up afterward, making sure that the color mix is exactly the same.

The Easel

An easel holds the canvas upright and firmly in place so that the artist can apply paint without accidentally touching it with his or her hands or sleeves, as would be likely when working on a flat surface. It also makes it possible for the artist to see both the painting and the scene or model at the same time and from the same angle.

The example on the right shows a box easel, while the example at the top of the facing page shows a radial easel. In the studio, the latter can be set up with the model or objects placed so that the artist can see them without having to move their gaze from the painting too much.

The box easel is shown erected outdoors in order to paint a landscape. The easel has sections to hold paints, brushes, and mediums, and even the palette if required, although in this picture the artist is holding the palette in her left hand.

The legs of the box easel can also be shortened to enable the artist to change their viewpoint and work sitting down. I prefer to paint standing up, but many artists like to be seated. Whichever you choose, remember to stand back periodically to view your painting from a greater distance.

TECHNIQUES

You are ready to start. With all your equipment to hand and some knowledge of how to use it, you now you have the challenge of actually applying paint to a blank surface. You may already have some experience with other mediums, but even so, many artists find a first encounter with oils and canvas—the materials used by the old masters—somehow more daunting. In fact, because you can scrape or wipe off oils, or simply paint over your mistakes, you will find them a very forgiving medium.

Laying a Ground

Most artists don't like to paint directly onto a white canvas because the intensity of the contrast between the canvas and the colors as they are applied make it difficult to work out the balance of tones. To avoid this, they usually cover their canvas with a neutral midtone color, such as a brown or greenish-gray. This is known as a base color or "ground."

I covered a canvas board with a thin layer of Burnt Sienna (left), which is the base color that I often use before painting. It has to be left to dry before work can begin, which with alkyd oils is about 12 hours. Other oil paints take longer, but you can also use acrylic paint as an under surface as long as you don't apply it thickly.

The color of the ground will influence the final painting. In the examples here, I've painted this surface (right) with Terre Verte, which is a cool gray-green, the second with Burnt Sienna (top of facing page), and the last with a dark color made by mixing French Ultramarine and Burnt Umber (bottom of facing page). So the first example has a cool background, the second a warmer background, and the last a very dark background.

30

When the base color had dried, I painted a still life of five lemons in a green bowl, first outlining the shapes in a dark tone, then blocking in the main colors with quite thick paint.

I used exactly the same colors for all three versions. These paintings are not finished—they are just a first attempt to show the colors of the objects correctly.

What is immediately noticeable is that the three pictures are all subtly different: the first looks rather cool in color, the second is much warmer, and the third appears more luminous. This is due to the background colors, which show through the paint and give a particular look to the picture. So you can influence the look of your painting from the outset, simply by the color of the ground you choose.

Of course to finish the paintings, I would add more layers of paint and start to show more detail in the fruit and the bowl, which would have the effect of diminishing some of the intensity of the base color. This means that eventually the three pictures would become more similar, but the base color would still have a subtle effect on the final result.

31

Drawing with a Brush

Once I have laid a ground, I draw an outline of the scene I plan
to paint using a brush—usually a small hog's bristle brush.
At this stage I try to make sure that all the main shapes are in
proportion and in the right place on the canvas. I can then
start painting immediately onto the framework created by my
simple outline drawing.

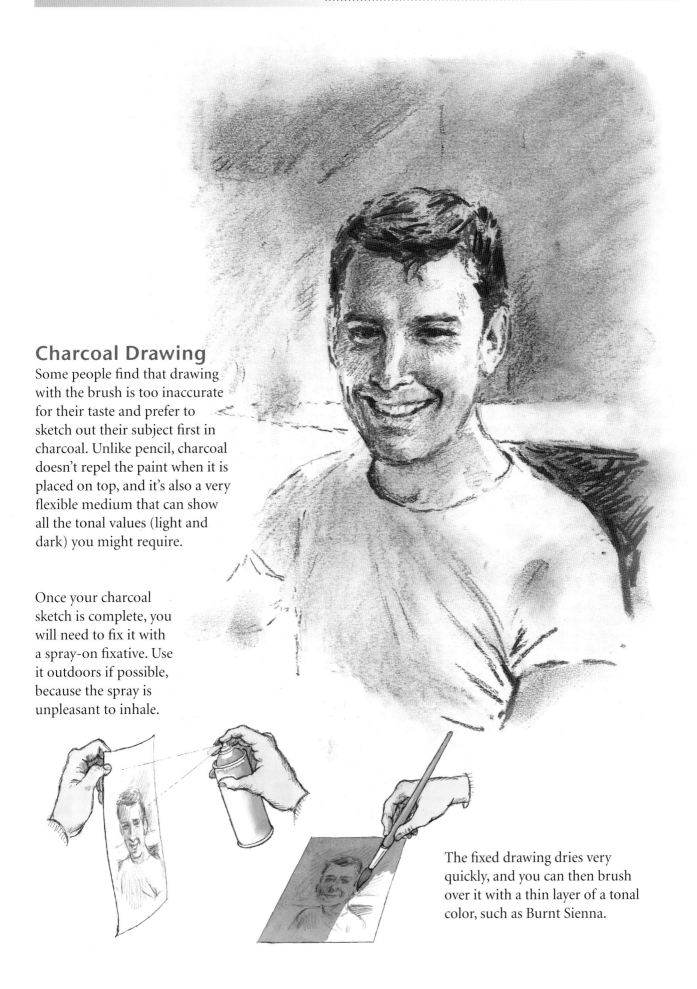

Charcoal Drawing

Some people find that drawing with the brush is too inaccurate for their taste and prefer to sketch out their subject first in charcoal. Unlike pencil, charcoal doesn't repel the paint when it is placed on top, and it's also a very flexible medium that can show all the tonal values (light and dark) you might require.

Once your charcoal sketch is complete, you will need to fix it with a spray-on fixative. Use it outdoors if possible, because the spray is unpleasant to inhale.

The fixed drawing dries very quickly, and you can then brush over it with a thin layer of a tonal color, such as Burnt Sienna.

33

Underpainting

A traditional but very painstaking way to prepare a painting is to render the whole subject in Terre Verte—a soft grayish-green—and show it in complete detail, building up the color until you have a tonal drawing in paint. You will have to allow it to dry completely before you can start the painting properly.

The time spent in developing your work is one of the reasons why an oil painting can take some time overall to complete. Quite often the tonal painting is then covered by a translucent layer of color, usually in an opposite color value, such as Burnt Sienna.

Squaring Up

When painting on location, always consider the possibility that you may want to produce a larger painting of the same scene at home afterward. This means that you must think about how much information you should put into the work you make on location in order to make a larger painting successful; it may be necessary to do more than one version of the smaller picture and some extra drawing and painting too.

Let us assume that you have returned from your outdoor expedition with a couple of small paintings and drawings as information and notes of color. First you must square up the piece of work that you are going to base the bigger painting on. Decide how large your squares must be to make an adequate grid to cover the painting. In the example shown there are five squares vertically and eight squares horizontally, making 40 squares in all. In the format of the picture shown, this is an adequate grid with which to work.

Next, transfer the image to a larger format. Begin by drawing the grid much enlarged onto the canvas but in the same proportion, that is, five squares deep and eight squares from side to side. Carefully copy the outline of all the shapes in the small picture onto the large canvas, square by square, until you have a recognizable outline drawing of your scene. Now start to paint in all the colors as closely as possible to those you recorded in your sketches. Your memory will also help you start to reconstruct the look and feel of the scene. To make the picture look as natural as possible, be careful not to tidy up areas of the scene too much, which is tempting when working on a larger scale.

To demonstrate how this works I've shown the painting almost finished with the squares still showing, but of course as you paint over the grid it will gradually disappear. Notice how the original squared-up picture is attached to the canvas, though usually it will only be needed during the first stages.

After you've completed your picture to the best of your ability, it's a good idea to have another look at the location to see if what you have produced has something of the essence of the real scene. It doesn't matter if you haven't got everything right, as long as it has at least one of the qualities that led you to want to paint the scene in the first place. If it has several of the qualities, you are doing very well. If you painted the scene again some time later, you would find it quite new, and you would see a lot more than before. This is part of the fun of painting; subjects never become boring.

THE APPLICATION OF PAINT

There are many ways of applying paint in order to achieve the effects you want. Mainly, of course, it's just a matter of laying on the paint with a brush and trying to show what you want to express as clearly as possible, but there are quite a few technical terms for the various methods of doing this that you may come across when reading or talking about painting with other artists. Here are some of them.

Wet on Wet

Laying paint over or next to a color that isn't yet dry is referred to as painting wet on wet. In the example below, on the left I put down a mixture of French Ultramarine, Cadmium Orange, and Titanium White, and on the right, a mixture of Dioxazine Purple, Cadmium Yellow Light, and Titanium White. In the middle section I painted a mixture of Cadmium Red Pale, Permanent Green Light, and Titanium White, allowing it to mix in with the colors on either side to produce a gentle gradation from one tonal color to the next.

   If at first you aren't able to achieve this effect successfully, don't worry—you'll learn how the colors blend with each other as your work progresses. Oils are slightly more difficult than some other mediums to deal with at the outset, but soon get easier with practice and eventually this is one of the easiest ways to produce really subtle work.

| Blue/Orange/White | Red/Green/White | Purple/Yellow/White |

Wet on Dry

Painting wet on dry means allowing the first layer of paint to dry before you paint over it with another color. Here I put down a mix of French Ultramarine, Cadmium Orange, and Titanium White (below left) and Cadmium Red, Permanent Green Light, and Titanium White (below right).

   When both were quite dry, I painted the opposite mixtures of colors over the top of these base colors, brushing them out and allowing the under-color to show through a little. Applying any number of successive layers is another way you can change the look of colors.

Blue/Orange/White   Red/Green/White   Red/Green/White   Blue/Orange/White
under   over   under   over

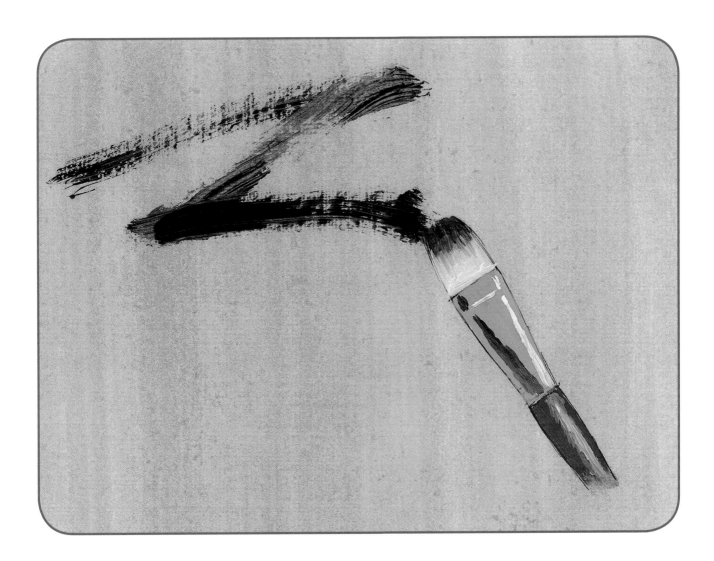

Dry Brush

As the term suggests, this is painting with a brush that is as dry as
possible. The marks made using this technique give the impression
of a stroke with a piece of chalk or a crayon. It is achieved
by making sure that the paint used is not loaded with oil—if
necessary, brush out the paint a little on another surface first.

Blending

When working on wet paint, two colors can be blended together deliberately where they meet. It is quite a difficult process, so you will need to practice. However, as you become more experienced, you will find that you can use smaller and smaller brushes to produce more subtle blendings.

Reducing a Color

Colors can be reduced by mixing them on a palette, or they can be reduced as part of the painting. Here I've laid down a strong blue, red, and yellow, and then, with the addition of white, gradually reduced their intensity until they are very pale. You'll find it quite tricky at first to achieve a smooth gradation of tone, but with a little practice you will soon perfect it.

Glazes

Sometimes it is necessary to adjust a tone or color that has already been laid down. One way to do this is by painting a glaze of diluted color over the top that leaves the original color still visible, thus creating a new color or tone.

To do this effectively, make sure that the underpainting is dry—if it's still wet, the new layer of paint will pick up a lot of the original color and instead of a glaze there'll be a mix of the two colors, which won't look the same. The glazing color must be diluted sufficiently with a medium to avoid it obliterating the underpainting. It's best to use a glazing medium for this, as just reducing the color with turpentine may cause cracking later if the undercoat is much thicker. Alternatively, linseed oil can be used, though it takes longer to dry than glazing medium.

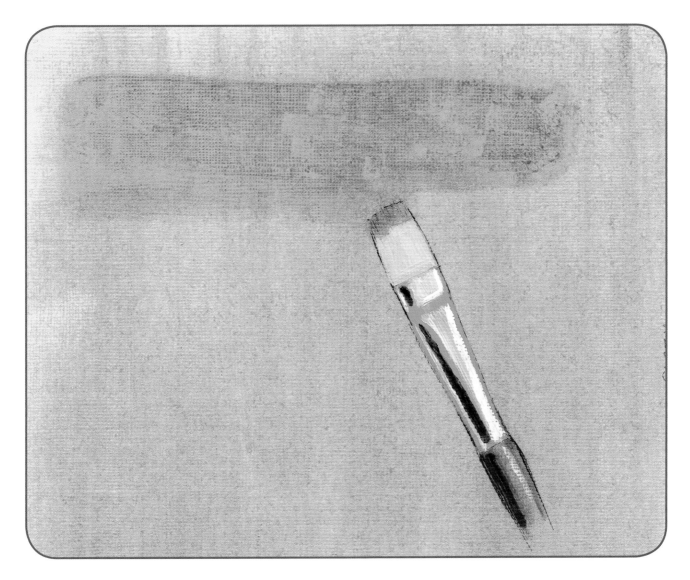

In the example shown here, the under-color is a thinned-down Burnt Sienna with a thin layer of Terre Verte painted over it. As you can see, the color of the Burnt Sienna shows through the Terre Verte to create a cooler version of the original. This technique is not difficult but will require a little practice before you become good at it.

Impasto

When working in oils, the paint is usually put on in a fairly solid way so that the underlying surface is obscured. In the technique known as impasto, the paint is applied so thickly that it shows the marks of the brush or palette knife and may even take on a sculptural, three-dimensional quality. It's an excellent way of adding vigor, texture, and expressiveness to your paintings.

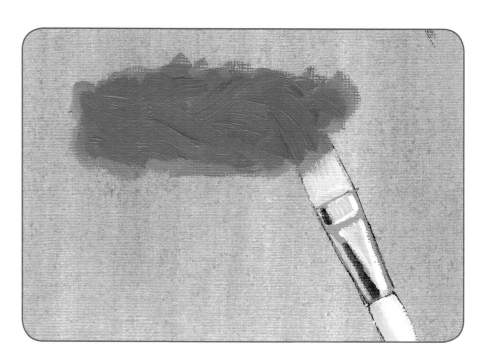

Scumbling

This term describes a way of putting a thin layer of color over another by pushing a bristle brush around the surface of the canvas, allowing some parts of the under-color to show through. It creates a sort of smoky effect and is useful for textures needed for painting landscapes in particular. In my example the under- and upper colors are both Burnt Sienna, but you can see how the tonality changes.

Tonking

This is a technique developed by the British painter and draftsman Henry Tonks (1862–1937). It reduces the thickness of painted surfaces so that they can be worked over further. Once Tonks had taken his painting to a stage where the paint was thick and still wet, he would lay a large sheet of newsprint across the surface, smooth it down, and then carefully peel it off again. This had the effect of taking off a thin top layer of paint in a patchy way, giving an impressionistic, broken look to the surface, which he could use to soften his more hard-edged work and create added atmosphere.

Some painters use newsprint, others use blotting paper or paper towels. If you experiment with different papers, you might produce some interesting results. The longer you leave a painting to dry, the more subtle the tonking effect will be.

Palette Knife Painting

Some oil painters don't like the highly controlled effect of the brushwork that most artists use and prefer to apply paint with a palette knife instead. This requires a slightly different approach to painting and creates a more impressionistic result.

Palette knives come in a range of sizes and shapes; the small ones have quite sharp points, allowing you to make fine marks. The marks they produce tend to be hard-edged, but they can be reduced by scraping with the point or edge of the tool. In the example below, I have used some French Ultramarine with Titanium White, but have not mixed the colors totally, so that the darker blue and the paler white show up, as well as the midtone.

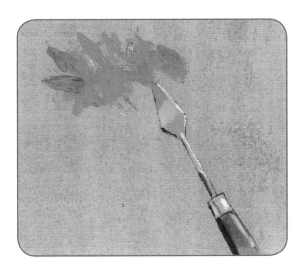

Portrait in Brushwork and Palette Knife

The portrait above is fairly conventional, painted with brushes of varying size and thickness. As you can see, the edges can be sharp and defined or soft and smoky. It's a method that can be taken to a level of photographic reality, depending on skill and the desire to paint in great detail.

The portrait on the right is painted in the same size, with the same lighting, pose, and background, but as you can see the effect is rather different. Here, no matter how much the paint is worked, it will never have quite the same effect as the brushwork. If the painting were a lot larger, the broken effect of the surface would be less apparent, but at this size part of the charm of the work is precisely the obvious texture.

CHAPTER 3

PROJECTS

This section of the book begins with still life, the easiest genre of painting for a beginner to tackle, although still life paintings can be just as powerful as portraits or landscapes. In still life, you decide exactly what objects you want to paint and you can take your time; the only occasion on which you may have a time limit is when you are painting flowers, but even flowers take several days to fade and die.

From still life we progress to landscapes, where it can sometimes be difficult to decide just how much of what you see you are actually going to paint. One way to choose is to make a frame of paper or card in the same shape as your canvas. Just hold it up in front of you and move it around until you see a section of landscape that catches your eye. Or pick an object such as a tree or building to stand at one edge of your painting and help fix the scene in your mind.

Finally, there is the challenge of painting portaits and the human figure. Since models are often only able to sit for for a certain amount of time, it's an area of painting where photography can be a real asset to record poses, and especially if you want to show a figure in motion.

STILL LIFE

This painting features several of the most popular objects used in still life, in very strongly hued colors. The composition is not without its challenges—the ellipse of both the rim of the jug and the bowl is an awkward shape to draw well, and the reflections and shadows on the fruit are key to their realism. This picture contains colored glass objects, but remember that clear glass is transparent, so if you place clear glass objects on a neutral surface or background, the colors seen through them will be simplified.

The whole composition is a mix of many colors against a pale background. Harmonizing strongly colored objects with a strong background color can also be effective—for example, if you have reds and blues, you might put them against a purple background, or in the case of orange and yellow you might choose a green background. Experiment with colors to get the best effect.

Stage 1

I prepared a ground of Burnt Sienna and drew the whole composition with a brush using a dark brown. If you are worried about painting straight onto the canvas, you may want to draw the whole composition on paper first in pencil or charcoal. You can then alter it until it is to your satisfaction. Trace if off and transfer the image to your canvas, then make an outline drawing in paint by painting over the lines transferred to the canvas.

Stage 2

The next step is to put in the main local colors. For simplicity I put in the background first using Titanium White with a touch of French Ultramarine and Naples Yellow, and then added the table surface in white, Cadmium Lemon, and a touch of Viridian. Then came the bowl in Viridian and Titanium White, with the mandarins in Cadmium Orange. The bottles were painted with French Ultramarine and white, and Purple Lake and white; the flowers are Flesh Pink and the leaves Permanent Sap Green. The top of the jug is a band of Lemon Yellow, followed by another of Cadmium Orange, then Cadmium Lemon mixed with white, and at the base Cerulean Blue.

Stage 3

With the bright colors blocked in, I turned to the main areas of shadow, including those cast across the background. The shadows on the wall and flowers are a mix of mainly Titanium White with a touch of Purple Lake and French Ultramarine. For shading the other objects I used the same mix but with some Viridian added and a little more white to prevent them from being too dark. The shadows on the foliage are made of Permanent Sap Green with French Ultramarine to strengthen it. I indicated where the main highlights were to appear with just a touch of white. Don't overdo the highlights; at this stage they are only intended as an indication that you will fill out more strongly later.

Stage 4

I next worked on making all the colors as correct as possible, including the darker and lighter versions of each object. The difference between the blue of the jug handle and of the glass bottle is a case in point—the former has more Cerulean Blue while the latter has more French Ultramarine. The purple glass bottle needed to be more blue, having started off rather red. I added a softer pink to the flowers and worked over the oranges with yellow and green tones and highlights of white and yellow, so that they aren't all exactly the same color.

Stage 5

Finally, I spent a lot of time on each object, putting in each bit of color and tone and sometimes making only minute marks with much smaller, pointed brushes. I found that at various points I had to lay thin coats of color over what had already been done, in order to get the exact tones and colors of the arrangement. In some places I had to soften the edges of objects and in others sharpen them up. One of the last tasks was to brighten or tone down the highlights and put in the very darkest tones on some of the shaded edges.

LANDSCAPE PAINTING

This is an attractive hilly landscape in the north of Italy, near to the Alps. It is both open and wooded, with large curves of hillside dividing the composition.

Stage 1

I started with a prepared canvas with a ground of Burnt Sienna and drew an outline, also in Burnt Sienna, of the main shapes of the view, keeping the marks simple and broad—there's no need to start putting in detail yet.

Stage 2

Next, I blocked in the main colors, taking care to show how much lighter the sky is than the rolling landscape, with its clumps of dark vegetation. The parts of the composition in the foreground are warmer in color than the parts in the distance. The colors I used were Cerulean Blue, Titanium White, Permanent Sap Green, Burnt Sienna, Naples Yellow, and Permanent Green Light.

Stage 3

Next, I put in the clouds and defined the vegetation, breaking up the grassland with marks in colors that start to give some texture to the surface areas. Note how the light falls on the trees and bushes, and remember that the marks you make in the foreground can be much bolder than those on the distant landscape. Once I was satisfied with the effect of texture as this stage, I moved on to finalize the colors and tones as below.

Stage 4

The final stage of a landscape entails carefully observing the way the marks that you make indicate the texture of the sky, trees, bushes, and pastureland. After building up the marks slowly, you can often smudge the surface a little with a brush or your fingers to get the right effect. Don't be too obsessive about the perfection of the marks that you have painted—experiment instead with smudging and laying glazes or washes over the finished surface and you may find exactly the quality that you are looking for.

After I had finished this landscape, I felt that the foreground should look much warmer, so I loosely washed a tone of Burnt Sienna and Naples Yellow over the whole of the foreground area and then smudged it lightly with my thumb until it looked just right.

URBAN LANDSCAPE

Painting an urban landscape is a little more difficult in practical terms because the space available in a street to set up an easel and work at a picture is usually limited. People passing by are mainly very courteous and tend to be appreciative of the efforts of the artist, but ideally you should find a place where you won't cause any obstruction.

The next problem is to decide how much of the crowded scene you want to include. A view along the side of a street where you can see the far end is usually good because there is a natural limit to the space, so that's what I've chosen to depict. The light in this London street is interesting—the buildings behind me are casting a shadow across the lower half of the street.

Stage 1

The first thing I did was to make sure that the perspective in the picture would work, so some careful drawing and measuring helped here. As you can see from the diagram (right), the vanishing point of the main lines of the perspective is not even in the picture, so a certain amount of guesswork was useful. It won't matter if your perspective isn't entirely accurate as long as the feel of the space is captured well.

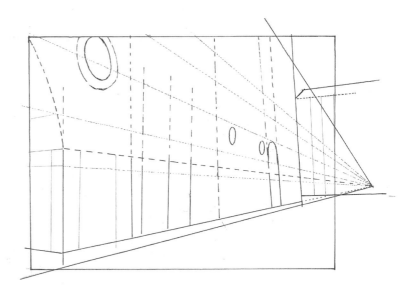

Stage 2

In this painting the buildings are partially in strong sunlight
and partially obscured by shadows cast by the buildings on the
opposite side of the road. This means that the lower half of the
buildings look much darker in tone and color than the rest of the
picture, so when I started blocking in, I defined the edge of the
darker shadow as well as all the obvious changes of color. The
lower half of the scene looks much darker than the rest, but I was
careful not to put in the shadow too heavily at first, because the
changing surfaces within the darker shadow needed to be built
up gradually.

Stage 3

With all the main color values established, I had to define the detailed shapes and various subtle color ranges within the overall context. I made the parts of the buildings in the foreground stronger in color and gave the edges of their hard surfaces more definition. I built up the darker parts gradually and tried to show more of the contrast between the light areas and the very darkest parts. The farther the buildings were from my viewing position, the less sharply defined the details needed to be.

FIGURE PAINTING AND COMPOSITION

When you're painting a human figure the essential thing is to convey the feeling of movement and, where there's more than one figure, to make a successful composition. The human figure is the hardest subject that you can paint; it's so familiar to everyone that it's easy to see when it's not correct. You need to look very hard at the disposition of the limbs and torso to show a convincing person. When you begin painting, it's advisable to keep your work less detailed to gain an understanding of the way a simple image can be more powerful than a complex one.

On My Bike

It's best to start with a single figure in a setting, and I chose this picture of my eldest son sitting on his motorbike to illustrate this point. I had to ensure that the combination of machine and human figure together were just right, so that the whole picture would make sense from the angle at which it is viewed. I photographed him first and then used the photograph as the main sketch for the finished painting since he didn't want to pose for very long. I also made some drawings of the scene to help with some of the details later.

Stage 1

Using a prepared canvas board, I sketched in the main shape of the figure and bike in Burnt Sienna. I also included some outlines of the background so that the scene was set for the painting as a whole.

54

Stage 2

Then I blocked in the main colors and shapes in a simplified way so that the whole composition was clearly shown in its color values.

Stage 3

Next, I began to work on the details of the figure and background, adding the darker and lighter tones to differentiate the qualities of the vegetation in the background and the leather-clad figure and the heavy machine in all its shiny hardness. This part of the painting was the most difficult—I had to make sure that the machine and the figure didn't blend in too much, despite both being very similar in color. I kept the brush strokes fairly broad, so that I didn't refine the detailing too much and lose the strong solidity of the shapes. In the final result the paint marks are still clearly noticeable, reducing the sharpness of the detail in favor of the strength of the statement that the paint makes.

A YOUNG MAN

When painting a portrait, the most sensible way to start is to take some measurements, especially if you are a beginner. You may feel it's a bit pedantic and delays starting the enjoyable painting process, but you'll find it really helps you to achieve a good likeness.

Stage 1

With a ruler or straight edge, measure the width and length of the head from your viewpoint. Once you have these measurements marked on your prepared canvas, note the position of the eyes, the end of the nose, and the center line of the mouth in relation to the top of the head and the chin.

It's also useful to ascertain where the center of the head appears to be from your viewpoint—in the example shown here, it more or less lines up with the left eye (left from our viewpoint). Making a few checks like this should enable you to portray the shape of your subject's head accurately.

Some artists start by marking in the eyes, followed by the nose and mouth, and then paint out from there to find the right shape for the face and head, but this can be difficult if you have never painted a portrait before.

Stage 2

I began by tracing an outline of the head and features onto the painting surface, using a small pointed brush. It's a good idea to keep the shape fairly simple and not worry too much about any details at this stage—you just need to get the main shapes and the position of the features right.

Stage 3

Next, I blocked in the main color values, aiming to get the midtone of the colors right. If you find that too hard, go for the darker tones—with oil paint it's always easier to paint light over dark rather than the other way around. Try to replicate the warmth or coolness of the colors and how they contrast with each other. As you can see, in my example the background color is about a shade darker than the skin tone and much lighter than the hair and clothing. The jacket is a warmer, slightly purple color while the hair is almost pure Burnt Umber.

Stage 4

Here I worked in the main blocks of color, defining features and colors. Showing the changes of tone on the face itself is clearly the most important thing, and then you can start to get a feel for the background intensity and the main shapes of the hair and jacket. Take your time with this stage. It's important to get everything in the right position, so that the face starts to become recognizable. Small things such the shape of the eyelids and the changes of tone and color around the nose and mouth are worth spending time and effort on.

Stage 5

The final stage was the slowest and most important, as now I was refining the portrait so that it began to look like my sitter. Every mark you make at this stage, no matter how small, can change the look of the picture enormously. So keep working until you're satisfied that everything is as correct as you can make it, or even ask for an opinion from someone else since they will often be able to see things that you might have missed. Don't be discouraged if they come up with lots of suggestions for changes; it's likely that there will only be one or two small things that aren't quite right, but when corrected they will make all the difference. In the end, you are the one who decides that you've done all that you can, and when you reach that point, stop. If nothing is wrong, then it must be right!

SELF-PORTRAIT

The benefit of painting your own portrait is that you can take all the time you like. Use a large mirror that you can position relatively close to you, because the distance you are from the mirror is doubled when you see the image. Good lighting is essential, and if you want to paint a view that is more in profile you will also need two angled mirrors, such as you find on a dresser.

Take exact note of how you have positioned your head so that you can return to the same pose each time you look in the mirror. It's best to move your head as little as possible while you are painting, and if you can arrange your pose so that you only have to move your eyes, so much the better.

Stage 1

Starting with a canvas prepared with a Burnt Sienna ground, I began to draw my portrait. This stage is when you settle the angle of view and put in outlines of the whole head and all the features. Include any obvious background, but don't be too detailed about this—the main point is the head. As you can see in my drawing, I have put in the edge of my canvas and a suggestion of the ceiling and wall behind me. Keep correcting your work until you are satisfied that you have a good likeness.

Stage 2

Next, I blocked in the main areas of color and tone, keeping them as simple but accurate as possible. I put in a background of a greenish-gray, with the canvas edge in a warmer tone. I then blocked in the main flesh color, which is a warm browny-pink made with Burnt Sienna, Naples Yellow, and Titanium White. I put in the shadows on the face very simply, using the same colors but with less white, and added some tone to the hair.

To take the painting to the next stage I darkened the areas around the eyes, nostrils, and mouth, and the shadows under the chin and near the hairline. At this stage your own painting should be beginning to look a bit like you, but should still be very simple.

Stage 3

Then I worked on all the subtle color variations on the surface of the skin until it began to resemble the color and tonal value of the face in the mirror, and the modeling of the features was clear. The highlights were put in next to give an idea of the contrast between the darker parts of the picture and those that are the brightest lit. Once this stage is finished, you should have a good likeness of your head, still rather impressionistic, although all the form should be obvious.

Stage 4

The last stage was where I really had to concentrate hard. Once the paint had dried, I slowly and carefully added variations of the colors until the rougher marks began to merge into each other and started to resemble real human flesh. Don't forget to work on the background as you go or the tone and color will become unbalanced. Everything should be starting to look much more realistic now, and this means emphasizing some parts and toning down others. As always, keep stepping back from the canvas to see the work at more of a distance, so that it's easier to check which colors to use. Sometimes you will only be putting tiny streaks of paint on the canvas in order to get the right quality of tone and color. Don't give up until you can't see any more that needs to be done.

61

GLOSSARY

Alkyd medium A synthetic-based medium, such as Liquin. Alkyd mediums add transparency to oil paints and help the paint to flow and to dry faster than traditional mediums such as linseed oil.

Alkyd oil paints Paints manufactured with alkyd resin, rather than a traditional substance such as linseed oil. These flow more easily, are more translucent, and dry more quickly than traditional oil paint.

Block in To paint blocks or areas of solid color.

Color value The light or dark quality of a color. For example, yellow has a very light color value.

Complementary colors Colors opposite each other on the color wheel, which make grays and browns when mixed.

Define To add clarity and distinctness of detail or line.

Dilutant *See* Thinner.

Ellipse An oval shape, such as the rim of a bowl when viewed from the side.

Ferrule The part of a paintbrush that secures the hairs of the brush to the handle.

Fixative A substance (usually a liquid in the form of a spray) applied to an artwork to preserve it or to prevent it from smudging.

Gesso A white paint mixture used to prepare a support (*see* Primer).

Glaze A thin, transparent layer of paint applied over a more opaque layer of dry paint. The glaze modifies the color of the paint beneath and adds depth.

Ground A base color or coat of paint (or other substance) used over a support to prepare it for painting.

Hue In painting, the attribute of a color that enables it to be classed as that color. "Hue" and "color" are often used interchangeably.

Impasto A technique where paint is applied very thickly, often so that the brush strokes or palette knife marks are clearly visible.

Intensity The strength of a color, which is determined by the amount of the dominant hue.

Linseed oil A natural oil, frequently used as a medium.

Mark In oil painting, the mark made on a support with an implement loaded with paint, typically a brush or a palette knife. Marks can range from tiny dots to broad strokes.

MDF (medium density fiberboard) An engineered wood consisting of separated fibers used as a support.

Medium A substance used to change the consistency of paint, usually to make it flow more easily.

Perspective The representation on a flat surface of a three-dimensional image as seen by the eye, to give the illusion of distance and depth.

Plywood A panel made of thin sheets of wood veneer used as a support.

Primary color A color (red, yellow, or blue) that cannot be obtained by mixing together other colors; but primary colours can be mixed together to make other colors.

Primer A substance, such as gesso, used to prepare a surface for painting. It protects the support and provides a key to which the paint can adhere.

Reduce To lighten a color, or make it paler.

Scumbling The technique of applying paint in a thin or broken way so that some of the paint that is beneath shows through.

Secondary color A color made by mixing together two primary colors.

Shade In painting, a shaded color is one that has been darkened, usually by adding black.

Size A substance added to paper during manufacture to make it less absorbent. Also a substance added to a support to seal it to prevent paint seeping into it.

Solvent A substance (such as turpentine) used to thin oil paint and clean brushes.

Still life A painting of an arrangement of inanimate objects.

Tertiary color A color made by mixing together primary and secondary colors.

Tone The lightness or darkness of a color.

Support A general term for the surface on which you paint, such as canvas, board, or paper.

Squaring up A method of scaling up a small image and reproducing it in a larger size, enabling it to be reproduced faithfully and in the same proportions.

Thinner A solvent used to dilute oil paint.

Tint A color that has been lightened, usually by adding white paint.

Tonking The technique of removing excess paint with a layer of absorbent paper such as newsprint.

Turpentine A strong-smelling solvent used to thin oil paint and help clean brushes.

Underpainting The initial layer(s) of paint.

Vanishing point The point in a two-dimensional picture where the receding parallel lines in a three-dimensional scene seem to meet.

Varnish A substance painted over the surface of a picture once it is fully dry, i.e. at least 6 months to a year after it has been completed. Varnish protects the paint and brings out the richness of the colors.

Wash A very thin layer of paint well diluted with solvent applied over a layer of dry paint.

FURTHER READING

Brindley, Robert. *Painting Landscapes in Oils.* Crowood Press, 2012.

Cuthbert, Rosalind. *Oil Painter's Pocket Palette.* North Light Books, 1993.

Friel, Michael. *Still Life Painting Atelier: An Introduction to Oil Painting.* Watson-Guptill, 2010.

Galton, Jeremy. *The Encyclopedia of Oil Painting Techniques.* Search Press, 2001.

Gorrell, Kitty. *Achieving Depth & Distance: Painting Landscapes in Oils.* North Light Books, 2008.

Gorst, Brian. *The Complete Oil Painter.* Watson-Guptill Publications, 2003.

Gregory, Noel. *Flowers in Oils* (Step-by-Step Leisure Arts). Search Press, 2001.

Kedzierski, Alex. *Artistic Secrets to Painting Tonal Values.* North Light Books, 1999.

Kessler, Margaret. *Painting Better Landscapes.* Watson-Guptill Publications, 1992.

Kreutz, Gregg. *Problem Solving for Oil Painters.* Watson-Guptill Publications, 1997.

Lang, Roy. *Roy Lang's Sea & Sky in Oils.* Search Press, 2007.

Macpherson, Kevin D. *Fill Your Paintings with Light and Color.* North Light Books, 1997.

Metzger, Phil. *The Art of Perspective: The Ultimate Guide for Artists in Every Medium.* North Light Books, 2007.

Moran, Patricia. *The Oil Painter's Ultimate Flower & Portrait Companion.* International Artist Publishing, 2000.

Nelson, Sherry C. *Painting Songbirds with Sherry C. Nelson: 15 Beautiful Birds in Oil.* North Light Books, 2007.

Pech, Arleta. *Radiant Oils: Glazing Techniques for Paintings that Glow.* North Light Books, 2010.

Philcox, Theodora. *Still Life in Oils: An Artist's Insight into the Creative Process.* AVA Publishing, 2002.

Powell, William F. *Oil: Cloud and Skies.* Walter Foster, 1998.

Roberts, Ian. *Mastering Composition.* North Light Books, 2007.

Robinson, E. John. *Paint the Sea in Oils Using Special Effects.* International Artist Publishing, 2000.

Saper, Chris. *Classic Portrait Painting in Oils.* North Light Books, 2012.

Sarback, Susan. *Capturing Radiant Light & Color in Oils and Soft Pastels.* North Light Books, 2007.

Serrano, Frank. *Plein Air Painting in Oil* (Artist's Library Series). Walter Foster, 2002.

Tolley, Elizabeth. *Oil Painter's Solution Book: Landscapes.* North Light Books, 2007.

Wileman, Peter and Allsop, Malcolm. *Painting Light in Oils.* Batsford, 2011.

Willis, Fritz. *Oil: Faces & Features.* Walter Foster, 1997.

INDEX

B
base color 30–31, 36
blending 38, 55
boards 12, 14, 15, 25
brights 10
bristle brushes 8–9, 40
brush drawing 32
brushes 6, 8–10, 15, 26, 28, 29, 32, 36,
    37, 38, 40, 41, 44, 49, 56

C
canvas 8, 11, 14, 15, 23, 25, 26, 28,
    29, 30, 32, 35, 40, 42, 44, 54, 55, 56,
    60, 61
charcoal drawing 33, 44
cleaning brushes 8, 28
color composition 16–19
color intensity 22, 30, 31, 38, 58
color ranges 18–19, 24, 52
color reducing 38, 39
color temperature 20–21
complementary colors 17, 24–25

D
dry brush painting 37

E
easels 6, 15, 29, 50
equipment 6, 8–15, 26, 28–29

F
fan-shaped brushes 10
figure painting 54–55
Filbert brushes 9
flat brushes 8, 9, 10

G
glazes 13, 26, 39
ground laying 26, 30–31, 32, 48,
    49, 60

H
hue 22, 44

I
impasto 40

L
landscape painting 21, 29, 48–57
    hillside landscape 48–49
    urban landscape 50–53
light 15, 21, 33, 49, 50, 51, 57
lighting 15, 41, 60
linseed oil 13, 39

M
mahl stick 11, 28
masking tape 29
materials 6, 8–15, 30
mediums 13

P
paint application 8, 11, 12, 26, 28,
    29, 30, 36–37, 40, 41
palette knives 11, 12, 40, 41
palettes 12, 23, 25, 29, 38
perspective 50
portraits 23, 41, 56–59
    self-portrait 58–59
primary colors 16

R
reducing a color *see* color reduction
retouching varnish 28
rigger brushes 10
round brushes 9

S
scumbling 40
secondary colors 17
self-portrait 58–59
shadows 21, 44, 45, 50, 51, 60
soft brushes 9
squaring up 26, 35
still life 31, 44–47

T
tertiary colors 17
thinners 13, 15
tints 22
tonking 40
turpentine 13, 39

U
underpainting 34, 39
urban landscape 50–53

V
vanishing point 50
varnishes 12, 13, 28

W
wet on dry painting 36
wet on wet painting 36